LONG ISLAND TRIPTYCH

SELECTED WORKS BY THE SAME AUTHOR

POETRY PUBLISHED IN THE U.S.A.

Dark Pavilion (Yale University Press, 1927)
The Tracing of a Portal (Yale University Press, 1931)
Winter-Burning (Alfred A. Knopf, 1938)
Long Island Triptych and Other Poems
(Alan Swallow & William Morrow, 1947)
Seventy Poems (Alan Swallow, 1965)

POETRY FROM IKUTA PRESS (KOBE)

Autobiography (pamphlet, 1971)
Atlantic Triptych (1971)
Double Triptych (1974)
Climbing to Monfumo (1977)
Walking Through Namba (1978)
The First Architect (1982)

LITERARY STUDIES

Lectures on Shakespeare (Nan'un-dō, 1958)
Shakespeare and Classic Drama (Nan'un-dō, 1962)
Studies in English Literature (Yamaguchi Shoten, 1982)

LONG ISLAND TRIPTYCH

Lindley Williams Hubbell

Afterword by Paul Rossiter

ISOBAR
PRESS

Published in 2025 by

Isobar Press
Sakura 2-21-23-202, Setagaya-ku,
Tokyo 156-0053, Japan

&

14 Isokon Flats, Lawn Road,
London NW3 2XD, United Kingdom

https://isobarpress.com

ISBN 978-4-907359-51-5

FRONT COVER

The front cover shows part of the *Shell Street Guide of Brooklyn–Queens*, published by the Shell Oil Company in 1940. It is reproduced by permission of the New York Public Library, where Hubbell was the librarian in the Map Room from 1925 to 1946.

CONTENTS

LONG ISLAND TRIPTYCH

one

GREENPOINT

I

The Glory of God shines over Greenpoint.
The oxen of the sun
Tread out the darkness along Newel Street.
The first stenographer announces dawn.
The delicatessens open. It is day.

II

Between Newtown Creek, Bushwick Creek, and East River,
Lies the green peninsula, the green point of land,
Covered with sea green grasses. The Canarsie Indians
Camped here for ages and in 1638
Sold it to the Dutch West India Company from whom
On April 3, 1645,
Dirck the Norman received the patent, whose sons
Sold it to Pieter Praa in 1684
And from that time until the public highway
Was put through in 1838, only
The families of Pieter Praa's daughters: Meserole,
Bennett, Provoost, Calyer, held the land
Where, in the fullness of time, Mae West was born.

The Russians, the Slovaks, the Hungarians
    and the Poles came.
It became part of the town of Bushwick.
The Italians, the Germans, the Irish and the Jews came.
Bushwick became part of the city of Brooklyn.
The refineries, the foundries, the warehouses and
    the gas house came.
Brooklyn became part of the great city,
The wonder of the world. At noon the sun is hot
On Winthrop Park, the colonnade and the angel.
In the side yard of St. Stanislaus the Polish boys
Are playing handball. Along Engert Avenue
From McCarren Park to Fidelity Memorial Park
The Glory of God moves like a procession
With gold fringe, black plumes, and muffled hooves.

III

The heart,
Said Rena,
Must learn to compose, like Palestrina,
Contrapuntally, for many voices,
Each one a separate part.
While one rejoices
Another sweats in anguish.

My dear,
Said Rena,
I suffer for you but I don't worry about you
Because I hear
The contrapuntal texture of your living.
Whatever mess you are in, that goes on without you,
Getting clearer and cleaner.

Essence,
Said Rena,
Is what matters. The rest
Is always either too little or too much.
Sight without touch,
Image without presence
Are good, music without image would be best.

I said
To Rena:
Who am I not to suffer?
I don't wish I were dead
And I don't need a buffer
Between me and hell.
I'm doing all right. I'm getting along quite well.

IV

The human heart is a great institution, I always say.
The prognostic attitude must be abandoned:
This cannot happen to me again cannot be said
Of love, nervous breakdowns, or artistic creation.
The heart of another is a dark forest, said Turgenev.
Who knows the human soul? said Emma Goldman.
You never know which moment will be your next,
said the woman in Dorothy Richardson.
The emotional as distinguished from the intellectual nature,
Says Webster's Collegiate Dictionary, Fifth Edition.
Behold thou art fair, my love, behold thou art fair.

The discursive faculty is a fool and a maker of fools:
Shakespeare is a barbarian, Whitman a slob,
Jean-Christophe sentimental slush, etc.
It loves nothing, it understands nothing,
it knows nothing.
It is in hell because it does not know it is in hell.
Hell is the absence of suffering.
Incapacity for suffering is damnation.
Indifference to suffering is death.
Give me an ounce of civet, good apothecary,
To sweeten my imagination.

The poet and the mystic are forever apart, but they are
friends and not enemies.
The poet aspires toward silence, the mystic achieves it.
The mystic has the firmer will, but the poet
Has the robuster appetite, he wants
To eat his cake and have it too. Hence confusion:
Duchamp turns to chess, Vaché to suicide,
Paul Valéry and Anna Hempstead Branch
To mathematics, Rimbaud to trade,
But none of them turned to silence.
Vivekananda cried out in terror, 'Where is my body?'

V

We see the Germans first in the austere
And lovely prose of Caesar's Gallic War,
On the first page. The Belgae, so he says,
Are bravest of the Gauls because they're near
The Germans who are bellicose, wherefore
The Belgae keep in trim. He says they have
No sacrifices and no priest who prays
To unknown gods, they worship sun and fire
And moon; in other words, what they can see,
The objects of their sight and their desire,
With no Druidic nonsense. Nothing save
Hunting and war concerns them. They are free.

In Tacitus we find them no less free
From Roman government and the austere
Stoic morality, but in him we see
More of their culture. They had all poetry save
The writing down of it (and they were near
The time of runes). This barbarous poetry prays,
Foretells the future and incites to war,
Extolls the magical excellence of fire,
Bays at the moon, howls at the stars, and says
Unspeakable things about the hot desire
Of earth at sowing time. All this we have
Only on hearsay, with its why and wherefore.

But these are modern things. To know wherefore
Man became upright, capable and free,
Behold the earliest German that we have:
Pliopithecus, who came so near
To being a full-fledged gibbon, never prays
To anything at all, is never austere
In act or concept, never wages war
Except to eat or breed. Anthropology says
He lived in the Lower Pliocene. Desire
Lay lightly on his shoulders. He could see
And think no further than he saw, could save
Himself from animals, but had no fire.

The next German may have discovered fire
(Homo Heidelbergensis); how and wherefore
We are ignorant. It is the tongue that prays
And that is lost forever, but we have
The jawbone and the teeth which are very near
To human. It is not likely he was free
From utilitarianism, the desire
For shapeliness in flints, for cooking and war,
Was probably far from him, yet he says
In this hand-ax from Saint-Acheul, that save
The proper human, nothing as austere
Had been designed, and it is here to see.

Next, the Ehringsdorf-Taubach man we see,
Proto-Neandertal, must have had fire,
Must have had manual skill, and seems to have
Aesthetic sense. He seems to have desire
For beautiful objects, witness these austere
And beautiful topaz tools, unfit for war
But exquisite to see. No doubt he prays
To the spirit of his prey, and conjures near
The animal ghosts. The primitive shaman says
The cave-bear and the sabre-tooth are free
Without his charm and fetishes, wherefore
The first priest signs the first contract to save.

The true Neandertal was human, save
For the higher arts; in his artifacts we see
A sense of harmony, the flint tools have
Proportion that could only come from desire
To make things comely. Abstract art is near
When the body is painted with manganese. For war
He fashioned axes. When the shaman prays,
He bears the cave-bear's jaw in his austere
And hairy hand. His imagination is free
From the grossest kind of fear. Familiar fire
Burns on his hearth perpetually, wherefore
He waits the lightning. He speaks
and knows what he says.

Ireland appears in the Mesolithic, says
Science, but there is little enough left, save
Some flints from Larne. The Mesolithic prays
No longer to the beast. The cult of fire
Flourishes and the sun is worshipped. Free
From the nomad's life, man now evolved the austere
Art of the potter, textiles for peace and war,
And microliths, to satisfy the desire
For beauty and utility, wherefore
The Maglemosean pointed bone shafts have
Them fitted in. Just at this time we see
The old age fading and the new age near.

As the end of the Neolithic age drew near
Came megaliths: dolmens, menhirs (which says
'Stone-on-end' in Celtic) and we see
Cromlechs and artificial caves which have
Blankets of earth covered with stones, wherefore
Great tumuli were heaped, for man's desire
To preserve the body was no less austere
Than it became in Egypt. Here he prays
To hafted ax and serpent, still not free
From chthonian terror, but the sun can save
The heart from darkness, and the friendly fire
Disperse the night and the nightmare of war.

Between the stone age and the bronze the war
Of metals passed through copper and gold, drew near
To iron and steel. Copper came first, wherefore
We speak of Chalcolithic, then the austere
And loveliest of metals, gold. Who says
Gold says Ireland. It covered it like a fire.
The Irish fibula spread to Troy that prays
To pre-Homeric gods, became the desire
Of all Europe. In the Iliad we see
The golden socket of Hector's lance. All, save
A little, came from Wicklow, duty-free,
And it was beautiful, and hard to have.

The first American Indian that we have
Is Folsom man. We see him first at war
With giant bison, peccary we see,
Sloth, camel, horse and antelope. Wissler says
He is Mesolithic, had the use of fire,
Was nomad, without pottery, with austere
Absence of decoration. Certainly prays
To something, limited use of bone, wherefore
He lagged behind Crô-Magnon. The desire
For durable baskets must have brought him near
To pottery but he never reached it, save
Possibly here and there: surmise is free.

The Poosepatuck Indians roam free
At Mastic where the salt winds blow. They have
Radios and have long since conquered fire,
Gas and electricity. They are near
Neighborhood movies, but the guide book says
Their blood is mixed with African, wherefore
The Shinnecocks, further out on the island, see
No reason to cultivate them, they desire
To remain unmixed, continuing the war
On racial tolerance. When will the austere
Voice of reason reach this island and save
The wretch who hates, the hypocrite who prays?

In Greenpoint only the broken hearted prays,
Prowling the streets at midnight, but the free
Frequent pool parlors, frequently they have
Tail in the park. The social worker says
They are a problem, being too dull to see
That only in this way they are able to save
Themselves from going completely nuts, wherefore
They are wise to warm themselves before the fire
Built in an ashcan, and to huddle near
Each other in the apathetic war
With death. Only when they are filled with desire
Are they beautiful, and in some strange way austere.

Who once was free and now is filled with desire,
Who burns in fire and can no longer see
To whom he prays, to whom he would draw near,
Cries out and says, it is better to have what I have,
To be thus at war with death, than to be the austere
Who know how to save themselves, who know wherefore.

VI

As I turned into Newel Street
The gas house smelled as plain
As when you were a child, and there
Was the old smell again,

And people that I never knew
Came crowding on the wind
Like drunken ghosts, their faces pale
Wavering and thinned,

But there was one who stood apart
And fixed me with a stare,
More beautiful than all the rest
And more than I could bear.

VII

The light that shines at the center of the universe,
The flame that burns at the center of existence,
The fire that glows at the center of my being,

The tranquility of Brancusi's bird,
Of Mondrian's great black and white diamond,
Of Debussy's clouds,

This is my home, this is where I live,
I have stayed away too long,
I must try to go back.

The wafers of triple bromide in the medicine cabinet,
The luminol, the phenobarbitol,
The codeine hangover,

The horrible dream in which you think you wake up
and find it is still true.
The fear of going to bed, the cup of hot milk,
The long walks at night,

The coffee in counter joints on Driggs Avenue
At four in the morning, the lousy sandwiches,
The dirty cup,

The hysteria, the clowning, the embarrassment,
the repeated pattern,
The renewed attempt, the discouragement, the shame,
The continued failure,

The humiliation of the mind, of the heart,
of the flesh, of the intention,
The taste of self-hatred sour in the throat
Like vomit,

The literary men who hate Shakespeare, the scholars
who hate life,
The artists who hate each other,
the bitching of one's friends,
The political row,

The religious crap, the mystic cult, the phony messiah,
The dull lecture, the frustrated and jealous women,
The fake experience,

The loud bullshitting in the pool rooms
and the bowling alleys,
The unfunny joke, the two packs of butts a day,
The bum liquor,

It is all good, I would not unlive a moment of it,
I do not disown a moment of it,
I thank God for it,

But it has taken me far from the center of my being
Where there is sound within silence and silence
within sound
And light within darkness.

I have been gone long enough. I have not forgotten
The way nor the direction. I shall go back
This time to stay,

And in that place where the air is unstirred
                    and untroubled
The wolves of confusion, disorder and excess
Will fall dead at your feet.

VIII

Anaptomorphus Homunculus
The tiny primate

Lived in North America
During the Eocene

Resembling the lemurs
Of Malaya

And the tarsioids
Of Madagascar

With short muzzle
And large brain

Before the ice sheet
Passed over Long Island

Before Pliopithecus
Chattered across Germany

Before Propliopithecus
And Parapithecus

Lived in the Fayum:
En ce temps-là le désert était peuplé d'anachorètes.

IX

Why are these people indifferent?

They are indifferent because they are ignorant.

But why are they ignorant? In every city,
Town and village there is a public library,
And though they are tired when night comes they are
not too tired
For radios and movies, for bridge and comic strips.
Why then do they remain ignorant?

They are ignorant because they lack curiosity.

Is not a lack of curiosity indifference?
Is this a vicious circle?

No.
Real indifference is knowing and not caring.
Lack of curiosity is not caring to know.
They do not care to know.

Emily Dickinson said,
My mother does not care for thought.

Precisely.
But why?

Because they lack imagination.
From lack of imagination comes lack of curiosity.
From lack of curiosity comes ignorance.
From ignorance comes indifference, or what seems

Indifference. Being without imagination,
No bomb is real except the one that hits them.

What can be done about lack of imagination?

That is the artist's job.

The artist has no job except to be an artist.
It is the educator's job to use wisely
What the artist has done.

It is the parent's duty to choose for teachers
Men and women with imagination.

But the parents have been corrupted by their parents
And do not care. Children are taught in school
To respect science but not art.
The grocery clerk laughs at the artist
Which puts the artist at a disadvantage:
An artist cannot laugh at a grocer's clerk.
Meanwhile science kills its tens of millions
Which art could have saved,
whether the artist wished to or not.

But under feudalism art was respected,
And without science men managed to kill each other.

To respect art is a great deal but it is not enough.
To understand art is to awaken the imagination
From which comes all the rest.

Can you make everyone understand art?

Why not? We have come a long way
From Anaptomorphus Homunculus.
When did the process end:
                    last night at midnight?

Who can set bounds for man's growth?
You must have the patience of God
In whose sight a thousand years are but as yesterday.
God can afford to be patient, I cannot.

I am not patient. I am a realist.
I do not expect a child three months old
To understand Beethoven's last quartets.

Then you have faith?

                                        Only in what I see.

X

In early middle age
There comes a quiet time
When you think the fight is won.

It has not even begun.

The fire roars in the wood,
The tide rises higher
Than you thought it ever could.

two

RIDGEWOOD

I

All the nine kinds of angels sing
Over Ridgewood in the spring,
The stoops are scrubbed, the steps are washed,
The pavements clean, the gutters flushed,
The boys and girls are dressed to kill,
The reservoir is on top of the hill,
The jive comes hot, the jive comes sweet
On Linden Street, on Linden Street,
And beauty sneaks up without warning
In Ridgewood on an April morning.

II

The Mespatches Indians lived where now in Ridgewood
German burgers drink beer, attend the Turnverein,
The Sangerbund, the movies, listen to the radio,
The English settled the Ridge
                    in the seventeen hundreds,
Looking down across Maspeth: English, Dutch, Quakers,
Ridgewood does not appear on Conner's map,
But in Beers' atlas it is a part of Newtown.
It now lies partly in Brooklyn and partly in Queens.

The houses are all alike but what goes on
Inside the houses is never twice the same,
Life being inexhaustible, or if the same
It is different in every person it goes on in.
Even to the same person love is different
Each time it happens, and the fear of death
Waxes and wanes with other circumstance.
Only the house fronts need numbers to be distinguished.

Crossing St. Nicholas Avenue you are in Queens.
The streets are broad, leaving plenty of space
For the sun to shine. Here and there an ailanthus
Splits its coarse orange bud and puts out green
As delicate as ferns. The romanesque
Church of St. Brigid stands at the borough line,
The German names on the delicatessen windows
Interrupted by pizzerias and olive oil.

The idiot boy and his brother, hardly more
                    than an idiot,
Go hand in hand down the street where a mind
As clear and cold as the ice cave of Amarnath
Writes poems, makes drawings, plays the piano:
The wind bloweth where it listeth. He said,
My uncle remembers when there were cows
                    all over Ridgewood.
When I was little he took me to the Grove
                    to the fights,
I can still remember how the smoke hurt my eyes.

III

Play Czerny to me. It says arithmetic,
Clearness with rapidity,
The passing under of the thumb,
Play it until your thumb is numb,
On you it looks good.

Play me the School of Velocity
With dispatch and ferocity
The way a woodpecker would.
Better play safe and play Czerny,
It says nothing at all.

Stick to Czerny. Above all
Do not play what Liszt made of the scene
Of love and death at the obscene
Height of the romantic movement.
This is all I can take.

I am hanging on the ropes but I know
They won't break
Because I twisted them myself and I know
Just how much they can take,
But it's better not to take any chances.

So play Czerny until your fingers drop off,
I'm a tough old bastard but there are limits,
And never mind your engulphed cathedrals,
Your gardens in the rain,
Or even the white peacock:
                                        I know when I've had enough.

Go up the scale and down the scale,
Let your thumb pass under and your fingers pass over,
And I hope to God I'm far away
When you learn to play
Beethoven.

IV

The true mystic has no truck with art,
The phenomenal universe being annihilated.
These atheists of art: Vaché, Duchamp,
Are like the American Association for
the Advancement of Atheism
Which meets on Sunday afternoon to denounce religion.
They are afire with religion. If they were not
They would be at a ball game or a movie, not there.
But mysticism annihilates religion itself,
Which is why St. Theresa got in trouble.
The mystics of art: Mondrian, Malevich,
Go only half way, end in a compromise.

The artist may be religious, but not a mystic:
Roualt is a great religious painter, Rembrandt a greater,
But mysticism is found elsewhere:
In the quiet of Quakers, the silence of Zen Buddhists,
The Nirvikalpa Samadhi of the Advaitins,
The Tao which if it is the true Tao is not the Tao,
Essenes, Quietists and Sufis. I asked a Japanese
Whose father was a Shinto priest if the Shintoists
Meditated. Yes, he said, they meditate all right.
Well, I said, what do they meditate on?
They just sit quietly, he said.

The Digambara Jains go naked and cremate themselves
Eventually, they wear cloths over their mouths
To avoid the slaughter of insects, at Ahmedabad
They have a hospital for wounded bugs.
Joseph Cornell put watch springs in a pill box
And dedicated it to Marcel Duchamp.
Art, religion and mysticism are confused
In this passion for purification and annihilation
That drove Rimbaud to Africa and
                    Walter Conrad Arensberg
To Hollywood, 'as far away from New York
As we could get without crossing the ocean.'

V

A million centuries before the first
Primate was born, a terrible race of creatures
Ran, jumped and hopped, in hunger and in thirst,
Across Long Island. Horrible to see,
Worse to encounter, they were the best of nature's
Efforts so far, which was enough to be.

A dinosaur's a noble thing to be
Compared with a trilobite. It was not the first
Nor was its fate to be the last of nature's
Experiments with life, but never were creatures
So large again. It is not hard to see
Why she abandoned them to hunger and thirst.

Yet out of predatory and sexual thirst
They produced an object which to this day can be
Admired for its beauty. It is possible to see
A spiral clutch of eggs, laid by the first
Armoured dinosaur, one of the creatures
Called Protoceratops. The art is nature's.

Elongated and ellipsoidal, their nature's
More like a bird's than a reptile's. All the thirst
For self-perpetuation of these creatures
Now turned to solid sandstone, they can be
Admired but not hatched. They are not the first
Vertebrate eggs that have lived for us to see.

From the Redbeds of western Texas we can see
An egg that is twice as old: in the course of nature's
Experiments in the Permian age the first
Reptiles laid eggs like this, the instinctive thirst
For continuance functioning as it was to be
World without end, in these archaic creatures.

In the Tertiary, among new fangled creatures
With wings, which had discarded teeth, we see
The Aepyornis' egg, which lived to be
Preserved in Elie Faure. This feat of nature's,
Like a Brancusi, satisfies the thirst
For beauty, while putting procreation first.

In the red sandstone of Massachusetts the first
Carniverous dinosaurs, sabre-toothed creatures,
Have left their footprints. Driven on by thirst,
They left attenuate marks for us to see
Like dried and curling leaves, preserved by nature's
Trick of petrefaction, which let them be.

Now in park and museum they can be
Examined at our leisure. We are the first
Of sentient beings to examine nature's
Enormous panorama and her creatures
With curiosity and intent to see
What appetite compelled them, and what thirst.

We are no different in our hunger and thirst
Except for our ability to be
At the same time objective and to see
What makes us suffer, having suffered first.
We are most helpless and most glorious creatures,
Being at once God's progeny and nature's.

After the dinosaurs had passed in nature's
Recondite procession, led by thirst
No less acute there came placental creatures,
Ungulate and herbiverous, to be
Ancestors of the elephant, the first
Mammoth and mastodon and bison we see.

Thus from original reptile to man we see
Inexorable intention, which is nature's.
The higher from the lower, the last from the first
Forever and forever, this subtle thirst
Produces from what is what is to be
In a succession of improving creatures.

Now on the streets of Ridgewood other creatures,
Placental and omniverous, we see,
Primates with tear ducts, and content to be,
For the most part, no other thing than nature's
Archaic and uncomplicated thirst
Intended them to compass from the first.

Who is not the first nor yet the last of creatures
Who endures thirst and bitterness, can see
That he is nature's, and is content to be.

VI

The room was grey before I slept
And white before I woke.
There were no human eyes that wept,
No human voice that spoke.

The sparrows sang their morning song,
The factory whistles blew.
I had grown wiser all night long
And ten years older too.

VII

My sister and I were in a train, crossing Siberia.
We could not see out the window, it was night,
But we came to a brightly lighted station and
the train stopped.
Oh look, I said, they have railroad stations here.
We got out and walked down a path, it was daylight now.
It was no longer Siberia, it was Italy,
And my sister was no longer my sister, she was
the Countess Anna.
There was grass on either side the path, and
beyond the road,
At a great distance, stood a group of monks.
She sang softly to herself, *Stell auf den Tisch*
die duftenden Reseden.
Ah yes, I said, what lovely music Richard Strauss
has written for those words.
Suddenly she left the path and, stooping in
the tall grass,
She picked up a little flask of Benedictine.
I laughed. You are as good as a St. Bernard dog,
I said.
The monks shouted and waved across to us.
Then we walked on until we came to a church
But it was no longer a church, it was a hospital
And the Countess Anna was no longer the Countess
Anna, she was my aunt.
We had come to this hospital to visit my mother
Because she was sick. We went in.
It was no longer Italy, it was America.
We started down a circular staircase.
I was filled with grief.
This is the trunk of which love is the leaf.

When we reached the bottom of the circular staircase
My aunt was no longer my aunt, she was Miss Brown,
A nurse, an old friend of my mother's.
I'm sorry, she said,
But your mother is having dinner,
will you come back later.
I started up the circular staircase with a
silver Persian in my arms.
Now in this place was a woman whom I did not know,
A malignant woman, my enemy. As I turned away
She slapped the silver Persian viciously in the rump.
I was filled with anger.
Who the hell do you think you are, I said.
Why, you practically hit my cat. She sneered at me.
Very interesting, she said, very interesting.
To get the reactions of a potential absinthe drinker.
I turned on her in fury. What do you mean potential,
I yelled, I love absinthe. Then I was rising in an elevator
And on the operator's stool sat a cat and over it
a sign reading:
IF ALL HUMAN BEINGS WOULD
BEHAVE LIKE THESE GENTLE CREATURES
THERE WOULD BE NO NEED FOR
A LEAGUE OF NATIONS
Ask birds how gentle they are, I thought,
and then ask worms about birds.
When we came to the surface the cat and I left the
elevator and walked off together
And a fussy old man followed us and kept asking,
Do you know this cat? Do you know this cat?
Don't be ridiculous, I said, we've known each other
for an hour.
This is the root of which love is the flower.

VIII

When the first amphibian lumbered
Into Ridgewood after supper
In the upper Paleozoic

The spore bearers and the gymnosperms
Were unable to understand
How animals could live on land.

IX

Why are these people malicious and full of hate?

Because they are unhappy.

That's not enough.
Take any two people who are suffering:
One grows in stature, the other turns to hatred
Of a race, a public figure, an unpopular movement.

The answer is still the same, they are unhappy,
But their unhappiness is rooted deeper
Than circumstance.

You mean a childhood trauma?

I mean a childhood fear. We hate nothing
We do not fear. They are inseparable.
We fear mortal disease and with good reason,
We fear our own inadequacy and failure
With less reason.

But feelings of inadequacy
Often result in bluster without malice.
Why do these people hate so bitterly?

Because they are afraid to love. They are afraid
To stick their necks out. After all,
it takes courage
To love. One is most vulnerable then.

But that is lack of courage and not fear.
The brave man fears the bullet and goes forward.

Call it cowardice then instead of fear.
The brave man sees love coming and doesn't duck.
The coward hides himself behind his hatred.

I think we are getting somewhere now. It is fear
That makes men hate, but not a general fear.
It is the fear of life itself, whose essence
Is love. I refer you to Dante and St. John
For the particulars.

What can be done about it?

Much by psychiatry, somewhat by religion
For the uncritical mind, somewhat by art
For the highly organized, a great deal
by experience
For the fortunate. The cures are many,
the disease is one,
But every case would have to be considered
Starting from scratch. Education of course
Could be a preventive but is hardly a cure.

Prevent a disease, there is no need of a cure.

Right. The more obvious kinds of hatred
Can be prevented by indoctrination,
But how about the petty and mean of heart?
No formal education can penetrate
To the obscure recoilings of the psyche
In early childhood.

A race of enlightened parents
Could cut those same recoilings to a minimum.

Right again, which brings us where we were
At the end of our last conversation, to wit:
Perfectibility of man, which is unproved.

I said I believe only in what I see.
I see that the diatom is no longer the highest
Form of life on this planet, I see we have come
A hell of a long way from the diatom.
Speaking of proof, have you any proof that the process
Of growth from diatom to man has suddenly stopped?
And if it has not stopped, when is it going to?
I believe in what I see, and I see no end.

X

Ask a bird about cats
Ask a worm about birds

Ask the heart
About worms.

three

GLENDALE

I

Sun and rain fall gently over Glendale,
The light is sweet
On 67th Street.

New moon and Venus glowing over Glendale,
And after dark
Desire prowls the park.

II

Glendale is happy because it has no history.
It lies between the cemetery and the railroad tracks
And nobody has ever written a book about it.
It first appears in the eighteen seventies
As part of Newtown.

The wind roars in the underpass entering Glendale,
All at once the houses are low and even.
The concrete cylinders of the coal company
Like the columns of Karnak stand above the tracks,
Egyptian and important.

Beyond the coal company the steel frame
Of the power station, with the sky showing through,
Delicately balanced, candid and reticent,
Resembles the Palace at 4 A.M.
By Giacometti.

In J. Wesley Drumm Park a glacial boulder,
Split in half, a bronze plaque fastened
To its wounded side, celebrates
A pioneer educator, for once apparently not
A contradiction in terms.

The necropolis stretches for miles with small pretentious
Marble huts for the useless dead, just as useless
When they were alive. The living live in rows
Of unpretentious and identical houses, who will be
Isolated in death.

The monument makers' yards are filled with slices
Of marble waiting for names to be cut on them,
Names of men and women and children
Now walking around Glendale, not suspecting
The association.

In the windows are pots of cacti and succulents,
With little imitation Japanese gardens,
Regardless of current hates, so strong the inertia
Of middle class taste, indifferently
Stuck into the dirt.

III

So you're going to take up water colors?
Paint a pierced heart with little fat-assed cupids.
Paint animals with long ears and with horns.
Paint someone who missed the boat,
Someone who hit the jackpot,
Someone with delicate strong wrists
And a long throat.

So you're going to take up painting?
Paint a locket stuffed with horsehair
And this inscription: Remember me. I should live so long.
The sky's the limit,
You can paint miniatures on ivory
Or you can be as strong
As Burchfield.

There's plenty to paint,
Don't worry about running out of subject matter.
You can paint fish on a platter,
Old women remembering
What it's like to get laid,
Or old men trying not to be afraid
Of dying any day now.

Paint someone with beautiful thighs,
And eyes
Like pebbles in a cold stream.
Paint a frustration dream
Of sculpture that melted in the oven
Because it thought it was terracotta
And it wasn't.

Paint Glendale in all seasons
And in every kind of light,
The green before a storm,
The grey during a storm,
The yellow after a storm,
Paint the roller skaters and the dancers,
Paint someone who thought he knew all the answers.

IV

Antiquarianism and the *dernier cri* are equally absurd.
A lyric by Herrick and Duchamp's valise are
equally valid.
The fear of eclecticism is unnecessary:
In my father's house are many mansions.
History is a room to move around in at one's ease.
Not the oldest or the newest but the most interesting
Should be one's concern, it is only thus one can be
truly modern
Because the present contains everything that
has happened so far.
There is no past, everything exists now.

The fear of eclecticism is bad but
eclecticism is worse.
You have to choose between Plato and Aristotle,
Between St. Francis of Assisi and St. Ignatius Loyola,
Between Pope and Blake,
Between Whitman and Maritain.
It is O.K. to take all history as your province
But you must make up your mind which city
you are living in.
You have to choose between the discursive mind
and the intuitive faculty
But you don't have to say one is nothing,
the other everything.

It's a question of having a center, that's all.
It's a question of being centripetal, not centrifugal.
You don't have to like everything you see,
                        but you don't have to be
Too snooty about what you don't like.
Above everything else, stand on your own feet.
It's the same with religion: in a decadent period
Religion becomes eclectic. When no one is on fire
With anything in particular, they start
                        combining the best
Features of previous faiths, producing a monster.

Nanak was the last one who attempted a synthesis
And got away with it. Today, all cults
That get to first base with the privileged classes
(The ones who can pay dues) begin by saying
That all religions are true. All cults begin
By saying, We are not a cult. We include everything.
I knew a man once who drew a chart
Of all human knowledge, and when he had finished
                        the chart
He thought he had acquired all human knowledge.

V

In the Devonian, Long Island was under water.
Fish were its most advanced inhabitants,
Appearing first, intent on love and slaughter,
During this age. Under the narrow sea
Crawled the crustacean, limited of sense,
And molluscs, contented not to crawl but be.

Majestically, where Glendale was to be,
The paddled Antiarchi cleft the water.
The jawless Placodermi, with less sense,
Were put upon by the inhabitants
Of this prolific and ferocious sea,
Having barely time to breed before their slaughter.

The acanthodians, as adept at slaughter
As sharks are now, had little else to be
Except eating or eaten, while the sea.
Deepened and widened, and beneath the water
Limestone was laid down. The inhabitants
Continued to grow in action and in sense.

In action more resourceful and in sense
More intricate, in breeding and in slaughter
Always more complex, the inhabitants
Of these fierce channels gradually came to be
Ready for the day when they would leave the water.
Some left it, others lingered in the sea.

Some of them to this day are in the sea,
While others, more evolved in mind and sense,
Inhabit Glendale. These who left the water
Have made an art of love, a science of slaughter,
And have developed things that would not be
Intelligible to the sea's inhabitants.

I that am one of the inhabitants
Of land should never have strayed so far from sea.
I would be better off if I could be
As sharp of instinct and as dull of sense,
As limited to progeny and slaughter
As these quick shadows in Long Island water.

Long Island water and its inhabitants,
Their love and slaughter in the shadowy sea,
The untroubled sense, are as they ought to be.

VI

Fall, rain, on my desire,
And on the earth
Tired out with summer.

For cooling only.
It is not the season of birth
Coming on.

It is death coming on.
Fall, rain,
On the cracked earth.

The earth is parched with summer.
I am parched with desire.
Fall, rain.

Heal the deep
Cut of desire's knife.
Make easy the passing.

VII

There are three stages of consciousness.
The first is waking, the ambiance of love,
The second dream, the subterranean source.
The life of animals is a perpetual dream.
The third is dreamless sleep, which we share
With minerals and the dead.
This is the impartial and promiscuous soil
In which our individual thoughts and dreams
Are rooted. Mystics call it Anima Mundi.
No Cretan snake god ever dug so deep.
Minerals live this life, which makes them beautiful
Whether in mountains or on museum shelves.
They are the quiet kingdom, living nearest
To the great soul of the world.

It is impossible to imagine
The unflawed purity of such an existence.
Love and its suffering, born of separation,
Cannot exist where there is no separation.
Religion ceases to have significance
Where perfect union has been achieved.
As for the negation of the phenomenal
Which haunts the modern artist, here it is.
Mysticism's dream is realized
Where the rain falls on granite, and neither rain
Nor granite knows that the rain falls on granite,
Nor granite that it is granite, nor rain rain,
Because such knowledge implies separateness.
This is the kingdom of the dead as well.
Those are pearls that were his eyes.

The marble and the man beneath the marble
Share one purity. Is it possible
To achieve this perfection without dying
Or being a mineral? Buddha says it is.
Confucius says, At fifteen I wanted to learn.
At thirty I stood on my own feet.
At forty my doubts were destroyed.
At fifty I knew the will of God.
At sixty my ears accepted tranquilly
Whatever they heard.
At seventy I could do as I pleased without sinning.

VII

In the Cambrian
Before the fish came

Radiolarian
Arrow worm

Trilobite
Limpet

Jelly fish
And sponge

Inhabited
Greenpoint

Ridgewood
And Glendale

IX

Why are these people cruel?

Because they fear being hurt.
It is a matter of pride
And strategy of defense
To get in the first blow.
Some bitter need of importance
Is satisfied by this.

But how then explain
Their contempt for gentleness
When their need of it
Leads them to cruelty?

That is their pride again.
He who defends himself
Despises him who won't,
Despises him who can't,
It is all the same to him
Whether he can't or won't.

He does it without hate.

We are all one of two things,
Sadists or masochists.
The masochist is the tougher
In the long run,
That is what is meant
By passive resistance.

But the passive resister
Is strong only because
He is one by his own choice.

Because he is masochistic.
His self respect is subtler
Because it survives defeat,
Because it grows by defeat.
The sadist has to win
Or acknowledge himself a failure.
Mussolini trampled
In Milano streets
Is obviously a failure,
Hypatia, torn with shells
In Alexandria,
Successful to the last.

Pity the cruel then,
The terribly vulnerable
Who build pathetic shelters
Of unkind words and acts.

Pity those who love them,
Who win out in the end.

Pity them both alike.

X

The voice of the ocean will be the same,
year in and year out
The stars will not alter their appearance
in the night sky.
The heart is stronger than anything that
can happen to it.

AFTERWORD

THE POETICS OF SIMULTANEITY: HUBBELL, STEIN AND CUBISM

The American poet Lindley Williams Hubbell (1901–1994) led a double life. Usually this implies living two lives simultaneously, one public and acknowledged and the other at least to some extent clandestine, but in Hubbell's case he lived them openly and consecutively. His first life, apart from short visits to Canada in 1932 and 1937, some months in Italy in 1935 and a few more in Puerto Rico in 1940, was spent in the United States, mostly in New York, where he worked as a librarian in the Map Room of the New York Public Library (1925–1946), and in Hartford, Connecticut, where he was born and brought up, and later taught (1946–1953). His second life began in 1953, when he arrived in Japan at Yokohama en route to Kyoto, where he had been offered a job cataloguing the library at the Zen temple of Daitoku-ji and was then offered a teaching position at Dōshisha University. He found that he enjoyed life in Japan so much that he never left the country again and in 1960 took Japanese citizenship and the Japanese name Hayashi Shūseki.[1]

Hubbell's life in the two countries was very different, especially in terms of his sense of well-being. In an interview conducted not long before his death in 1994, he told Yoko Danno, his friend and Japanese publisher, 'I always feel more at home here than I ever felt in America.... Every day I give thanks that I am in Japan' ('Interview', 58). There was, however, a thread that tied his two lives together, and this was literature, in the form of drama and especially of poetry. His engagement with drama began early: he told Yoko Danno that between the ages of eight and ten he read and fully memorised his mother's edition of the complete works of Shakespeare ('Interview,' 58). Much of his university teaching in Japan was concerned with drama, especially Shakespeare, as were his two most important works of literary criticism, *Lectures on Shakespeare* (1958) and

Shakespeare and Classic Drama (1962), both published in Tokyo. He also became a connoisseur of nō theatre: according to a list he made for Yamamoto Shigeki in 1978, in his first twenty-five years in Japan he had attended no fewer than 849 performances of 186 different plays.

It was poetry, however, that was the strongest thread linking his two lives, and it was his sense of himself as a poet that was most central to his identity. His career began well when his first book, *Dark Pavilion*, received a Yale Younger Poets award and was published by Yale University Press in 1927; Yale went on to publish his second book, *The Tracing of a Portal,* in 1931. When Alfred A. Knopf brought out *Winter-Burning*, his third book, in 1938, Hubbell joined a prestigious list that included Elinor Wylie, Wallace Stevens, A. E. Housman, and Witter Bynner. His fourth book, *Long Island Triptych and Other Poems*, whose title poem is reissued here, was published by George Morrow and Alan Swallow in 1947, and his final American-published volume, *Seventy Poems*, containing work from both the U.S. and Japan, was published by Alan Swallow in 1965. From then on, Hubbell's poetry – including five further full-length volumes, the last of them appearing in 1982 – was published almost exclusively by Yoko Danno's Ikuta Press in Kobe.

Hubbell's style changed radically during the course of the fifty or sixty years of his writing life. His first two books are very much a product of their era: the poems are short, lyrical, highly personal, deftly rhymed, and finely cadenced – much in the style of 1920s New York poets such as Elinor Wylie, Edna St. Vincent Millay or Louise Bogan. His range, emotionally, technically, and in terms of content, widens a little in his second book and then considerably more in *Winter-Burning* of 1938, but there is little sign of the influence of the modernism of William Carlos Williams, Wallace Stevens, or Marianne Moore that was equally a feature of New York poetry in the 1920s. It is not until the poems he wrote after 1938 and published in *Long Island Triptych and Other Poems* in 1947 that he enters his second period, one in which his poetry is marked by large-scale expansions of subject matter, reference, form and technique, all framed in an ambitiously modernist style. After this, his style continued to change and develop: in his third period, in line with his more cheerful and less stressed life in Japan, his poems tended to be short, genial, well-observed, and attractively focused on the local and the quotidian.

Long Island Triptych and Other Poems is, I think, the high point of Hubbell's career, and the title poem – forty-eight pages in the original edition, fifty-nine in this one – seems to me to be an important mid-century, mid-length poem, and one that has been unjustly neglected – perhaps slipping out of sight because of Hubbell's expatriation in the latter part of his life. The early and mid-twentieth century is rich in poems of roughly this length, ranging from modernist masterpieces by T. S. Eliot and the early Ezra Pound through to the 'sonatas' of Basil Bunting, along with mid-length poems by Wallace Stevens, W. H. Auden, Kenneth Rexroth, John Berryman, and others. Poems by these authors are in varying degrees modernist – Bunting very much so, Auden hardly at all – but *Long Island Triptych*, it seems to me, belongs towards the modernist end of the spectrum. Hubbell's modernism, however, is not like anybody else's: in its technical bravura, in its practice of juxtaposition (whether of forms or of subject matter), in its range and variety of reference, and in its overarching formal architecture, it is a strikingly original production. Hubbell was a great admirer – and good friend – of Gertrude Stein, and he was also a lover of modernist art ranging from the work of Cézanne through to the radical abstractions of Brancusi, Malevich, Mondrian and Moholy-Nagy. Even though *Long Island Triptych* is not like anything written by Stein, I think it can best be approached via Stein's literary works, especially *Three Lives*, and also through her writings on Cézanne and on Picasso's cubism.

Kenneth Rexroth defined cubism in poetry as 'the conscious, deliberate dissociation and recombination of elements into a new artistic entity made self-sufficient by its rigorous architecture' (Rexroth, 253). He goes on to distinguish this way of writing from, on the one hand, modernist poetry in which the primary elements of the poem are 'narrative or at least informative wholes' collaged together, such as Apollinaire's 'Zone', Eliot's *The Waste Land*, Pound's *Cantos*, or Williams's *Paterson*, and from, on the other hand, 'the free association of the Surrealists and the combination of unconscious utterance and political nihilism of Dada'. Perhaps a further contrast needs to be made with multi-part poems whose form is based on a musical rather than on the painterly analogy implied by Hubbell's title. Eliot's *Four Quartets*, in which each poem consists of five 'movements', features a counterpoint of four voices (Moody, 143-149), and states and develops opposing themes 'first falsely, then truly, reconciled' (Kenner, 312) would be one example. Basil Bunting's mid-length poems, such as *The Spoils* or *Briggflatts*, explicitly categorised by him as 'sonatas', would be further instances, with their Scarlatti-like deployment of first and second themes within a structure of exposition, development, and resolution (Gordon, 107-110).

Rexroth originally put forward his definition of poetic cubism in the introduction to his 1973 translation of *Selected Poems* by Pierre Reverdy, and Reverdy's practice – involving 'dismembered propositions ... restructured into an invisible or subliminal discourse which owes its cogency to its own strict, complex and secret logic' – is one form cubist poetry may take; others, he claims, may be found in Gertrude Stein's *Tender Buttons*, his own *The Art of Worldly Wisdom* (written in the 1920s but not published until 1949), and some of the early work of Laura Riding and Yvor Winters. Hubbell's *Long Island Triptych* is not like the work of any of these writers, but I shall suggest that one striking thing about it is that it can, in its use of repetition and recombination to create an overall architecture, usefully be seen as a cubist work: I don't think there are many other mid-length English-language poems of which this can plausibly be said.

§

It is difficult to overestimate the importance of Stein and her work for Hubbell. When asked by Yoko Danno in the 1994 interview which five writers were most important to him, he named Shakespeare, Ibsen, Homer, Emily Dickinson, and Gertrude Stein (65). This answer gives a sense of how much Stein mattered to him, as does his statement in his minimalist *Autobiography* of 1971 that his first reading of *Tender Buttons* was one of the three aesthetic experiences that, at the age of seventy, he would most like to be able to relive. This is further reinforced by a story told by Donald Richie, who, when given a similar list of favourite authors by Hubbell, asked about Gertrude Stein's being there:

> Of course, he said. She is very good. Then, perhaps noticing that I did not understand, he quoted the Koran: We make no distinction among God's prophets. (Richie, 4)

The first of Stein's works thar Hubbell read was 'Vacation in Brittany', a short three-part prose text published in the Spring 1922 issue of *The Little Review*. He then read *Three Lives* and *Tender Buttons,* the two books by Stein he found on the shelves of the New York Public Library; he was, he said, 'overwhelmed' (Interview, 62). At that time Stein was widely mocked, which led Hubbell to write a letter to Eugene Jolas, editor of the Paris magazine *transition*, praising Jolas for printing Stein's work; Jolas showed this letter to Stein, who wrote to Hubbell, saying, 'Mr Jolas has just shown me your letter to *transition.* It gave me a great deal of pleasure.' After this they corresponded regularly.[2] When Stein arrived in New York in 1934 for her first lecture tour, she contacted Hubbell, and thereafter they saw each other frequently when she was in America.

One of the early fruits of this friendship was the poem 'A Letter to Gertrude Stein', which appeared in *The Tracing of a*

Portal in 1931, three years before Stein and Hubbell met in person. The poem is not Steinian in style, but in its Whitman-like, almost Blakeian energy, it feels like something new – both emotionally and technically – in Hubbell's work.[3] A more important long-term consequence of his encounter with Stein and her work, however, was the way it helped him to arrive at his own idea of the longer modernist poem. He certainly knew both *The Waste Land* and *Hugh Selwyn Mauberley*, and both those works were in different ways influential, but it was, I feel, Stein's example that enabled him to arrive at his own very personal idea of how *Long Island Triptych* should be shaped.

In his essay 'Gertrude Stein: The First Period', included in *Studies in English Literature* (1982), Hubbell claims that Stein's *The Making of Americans* is 'one of the three giant monoliths of twentieth-century literature' and argues that, like the other two – *Ulysses* and *A la recherche du temps perdu* – Stein's book is at bottom 'a profound meditation on time'. He goes on:

> Modern literature is based on a new concept of time, derived from the post-Euclidean geometry and the post-Newtonian physics of Einstein and his contemporaries.... In the epics of Proust, Joyce, and Stein [and] in the poetry of Pound and Eliot ... you will find this new concept of time, for today time is no longer held to be an absolute, but a dimension of matter. (188)

This revolution in our understanding of time compels us, Hubbell claims, 'to abandon the idea of time as an enormously long yard-stick, and to think of it as a simultaneity rather than a sequence' (188). This was clearly a key idea for him: he returns to it a number of times in his critical writings about Stein, Pound and Eliot. Thus, in the transcript of his lecture 'Modern Poetry', given at Dōshisha Women's College in 1983, he explains the reason for the difficulties that readers – including his own students – have had with *The Waste Land* in these terms:

> I always tell my students when we start on *The Waste Land*, 'There isn't a difficult line in this poem. There isn't a line in this poem that you can't understand. It's simply the sequence that gets people.' ... People say ... 'What goes on? It's just all mixed up.' Well, that's what goes on. It's because of the new sense of time that we have in the twentieth century.... [A]ll you have to know to enjoy *The Waste Land* [is that] it's a simultaneity not a sequence. (8-9)

This description of *The Waste Land* sounds, as we shall see, rather like Hubbell's own portrayal of the mixed-up nature of 'what goes on' in the peaceful neighbourhoods of Long Island, where dinosaurs, German immigrants, Confucius, the piano music of Czerny, and the wind that 'roars in the underpass entering Glendale' coexist as differently angled facets of the compound nature of a neighbourhood.

However, as Hubbell points out in both his essay and his 1983 lecture, simultaneity is easier to achieve in painting than in literature, which of its nature exists in time:

> One of Picasso's so-called double profiles is simply the same face seen from two different angles simultaneously. They are superimposed. And probably the most important ... painting this century is Marcel Duchamp's *Nude Descending a Staircase*.... You don't see the woman and you don't see the staircase. You see a whole series of overlapping lines, curves, forms.... What you are seeing is every moment of her descent.... It's not a picture of a woman or a staircase. It's a picture of a descent. Now that's simultaneity.... Now, when you come to a poet, he has a different problem, because you can look at two things at the same time ... but you can't read two lines of poetry at the same time. So whereas the painter can superimpose, the poet can only juxtapose. (Dōshisha lecture, 9-10)

The use of juxtaposition in the service of achieving a sense of simultaneity is a key strategy in *Long Island Triptych*, and in this sense the poem is a work in the mainstream of the High Modernist tradition. Hubbell himself sees the focus on time, simultaneity and juxtaposition as being the key to the great works of modernist poetry:

> In the first [of Pound's *Cantos*] ... we find a curious and prophetic juxtaposition of Homer and his sixteenth-century translator, Andreas Divus. In *Mauberley* we have the juxtaposition stated explicitly: Sappho's barbitos and the pianola, Dr. Johnson's Fleet Street and a modern shopping district.... In the first section of *The Waste Land* we are in Central Europe and London soon after World War I, at the battle of Mylae which was fought in 260 B.C., on the ship that is carrying Isolde to Cornwall, while the voices of Old Testament Prophets, Dante, Webster, and Baudelaire, weave in and out through the shifting scenes. (*Second Miscellany*, 94-95)

In 'Angelology', the second of the 'other poems' in *Long Island Triptych and Other Poems*, juxtaposition had already been strikingly deployed as various orders of angels are seen as being vividly present in twentieth-century New York. The juxtaposition of dominions singing – 'with the tromba marina, or with continuo / on the clavicembalo' – with trucks waiting in alleys, or of thrones in flight with Tex Ritter on the juke box, is a striking feature of this poem: time is seen less as a horizonal flow than as a series of historical depths, all of which are felt – as in *The Waste Land* – to be simultaneously present and fully implicated in the lived experience of the contemporary city.

This use of juxtaposition foreshadows a key strategy of *Long Island Triptych* itself, but what is most striking about Hubbell's longer poem is its formal design. Hubbell had been, and always remained, a metrical craftsman of great skill, and when he came to construct his own large-scale modernist poem, he did not abandon his engagement with traditional forms but rather capitalised upon it. Like *Mauberley* and *The Waste Land*, the triptych is full of contrasts in voice, historical moment, register, and many of the other juxtapositions to be found in the master works of Pound and Eliot, but the poem's most fundamental contrasts are formal ones. Each panel of the triptych consists of ten metrically distinct poems and focuses on one of three New York neighbourhoods: Greenpoint (in Brooklyn), Ridgewood (in Queens), and Glendale (also in Queens). The three panels are perfectly aligned with each other in that they each consist of the same ten poetic forms deployed in the same order; the matter dealt with in these different kinds of writing is extremely various, but this variety of both content and form is contained within a robust structure of formal parallelism. Thus, not only are different people, species, works of art, religions, and historical – even geological – eras juxtaposed, but different poetic forms are similarly placed side-by-side in a way that at first seems arbitrary – in that it stresses the heterogeneity of the forms being used – but is in fact not haphazard in that similar forms appear in the same positions in all three panels of the triptych.

To make this parallelism clear, it may be helpful to describe the sequence of different kinds of writing in 'Greenpoint', the first panel of the triptych, so as to make plain the matrix to which all three parts conform. The first part of the poem begins joyously at the start of day in Greenpoint:

> The Glory of God shines over Greenpoint.
> The oxen of the sun
> Tread out the darkness along Newel Street.
> The first stenographer announces dawn.
> The delicatessens open. It is day.

The co-existence of the Glory of God, the Homeric oxen of the sun, the named suburban New York street, the stenographer, and the delicatessens sounds a chord that brings together different times, persons, settings, and orders of reality in an urban harmony, and in doing so announces juxtaposition and simultaneity as important procedures of the poem. This brief opening chord is then immediately followed by something formally different: a poem in (mostly) five-stress lines of geographical description and historical narrative running from the sale of the land by the Canarsie Indians to the Dutch West India Company in 1638 through to the construction of the modern refineries, foundries, and warehouses – and to local Polish boys playing handball in the side yard of the St Stanislaus Kostka Catholic Academy in the 1940s. Part III is a conversational poem in irregularly rhymed seven-line stanzas, a dialogue between the main speaker and someone called Rena, who plays much the same role as the person who in Venice in an earlier poem in the volume, 'Five Places', assured Hubbell of his sanity during a major crisis in his life by saying, 'No, Mr. Hubbell, you're not going crazy, / If you were you wouldn't ask me that question'; this time, however, there seems to be less need of reassurance as the speaker replies to Rena, saying, 'I don't need a buffer / Between me and hell. / I'm doing all right. I'm getting along quite well.' Part IV is a disquisition on the human heart, on the distinction between the emotional and the intellectual in human nature, and on that between the poet and the mystic ('The poet aspires toward silence, the mystic achieves it'), with a supporting cast that includes, among others, Turgenev, Emma Goldman, Dorothy Richardson ('You never know which moment will be your next'), *Webster's Collegiate Dictionary* (Fifth Edition), Duchamp, Valéry, Rimbaud and Vivekananda.

We are not yet halfway through the first panel of the triptych, but I think it must already be clear that the poem is replete with different perspectives, poetic forms, orders of information, allusions, tones of voice, and emotional emphases. This carnival of juxtaposition reaches a climax in poem V, which is a double sestina, one of the most demanding poetic forms in the western tradition. The basic sestina form consists of six six-line stanzas, in which the six key words appearing at the line endings in the first stanza reoccur in all the other stanzas in a strictly rotating order; the six stanzas are followed by a three-line coda using all of these six key words. The double sestina exists in two different versions, one consisting of twelve six-line stanzas plus a three-line coda, the other of twelve twelve-line stanzas with a six-line coda: the sestina in poem V of 'Greenpoint' is the longer and more challenging of these two variants. The writing in the four poems of the sequence up to now has been tight and well-focused, but this double sestina makes clear the degree of control Hubbell has over a difficult verse form which is being used to articulate the most disparate material. This material consists of no less than a history of mankind from various pre-Neanderthal species all the way through to the Greenpoint's contemporary inhabitants who 'frequent pool parlors [and] frequently … have / Tail in the park.'

This virtuoso performance, the longest poem in the sequence, is followed by one of the shortest, a lyric in three rhymed quatrains which takes us back to Newel Street to capture a moment of heart-breaking personal vision, and this is in turn followed by a tightly written, deeply personal poem about a recovery from humiliation, self-hatred, and bad living, and a return to 'the sound within silence and the silence within sound / And light within darkness' (associated with the work of Brancusi and Mondrian) that consitutes 'the center of my being'. Poem VIII is a plunge into prehistoric time, a brief poem in couplets about precursors to *Homo sapiens* that inhabited Greenpoint 'Before the ice sheet / Passed over Long Island', while poem IX is a dialogue investigating human ignorance and indifference and the role of art in awakening imagination. After all this multi-faceted matter, whose variety is representative of many aspects of Hubbell's life, thought, and preoccupations, the panel ends with a coda that leaves us with a sense of personal fragility, reminiscent of that expressed earlier in the volume in 'Five Places':

In early middle age
There comes a quiet time
When you think the fight is won.

It has not even begun.

The fire roars in the wood,
The tide rises higher
Than you thought it ever could.

The first panel of the triptych thus has a great variety of subject matter expressed through an equally great variety of formal procedures. The variety is in fact so great that at first sight there might seem to be a danger of miscellaneity – if, that is, the energy of the writing didn't keep propelling the poem forward with such vigour that the reader never has time to question where – if anywhere – the work might be headed, or how – or whether – it might achieve unity. ('You never know which moment will be your next.') However, the architecture of the triptych as a whole becomes clear when one moves to its second part, about Ridgewood, and then on to its third part, about Glendale. Each neighbourhood is described in ten poems, each of which employs a different form, and the sequence of forms is the same as that in the Greenpoint section. Any sense of miscellaneity thus fades on arrival at 'Ridgewood' and then at 'Glendale' as the architecture becomes plain, enabling a shift from a sense of burgeoning profusion to an understanding of how a huge variety of matter is able to enter the poem and be contained there without any item either losing its own quiddity or disrupting the architectural structure of the whole.

The variety of matter is in fact extraordinary: among new material in the second and third panels we find pizzerias and German delicatessens, Czerny, the American Association for the Advancement of Atheism, St Theresa, Mondrian, Malevich, Quakers, Zen Buddhists, Shintoists, Joseph Cornell, dinosaurs (and their eggs), mammoths and mastodons, sparrows and factory whistles, a dream of Siberia (which becomes Italy, which becomes America), unhappiness, imitation Japanese gardens, water colours, Robert Herrick, Duchamp's valise, the beauty of minerals, Confucius, and much else. The heterodox nature of these items, all contained within a form of great robustness, reflects both multiple aspects of the neighbourhoods referred to and also the curiosity, lived experience, knowledge – and quirkiness – of an observant inhabitant of New York.

After this festival of particulars the triptych ends, in the final short coda to its third part, with greater strength and optimism than was the case in its first part:

> The voice of the ocean will be the same,
> year in and year out
> The stars will not alter their appearance
> in the night sky.
> The heart is stronger than anything that
> can happen to it.

And the form is so strong that (it seems) almost anything can be contained in it.

§

Not just strong, however. The key points about this form are that it is multi-faceted and decentred: the multiple perspectives and formal variety are certainly held in a pattern, but there is no centre to the design that makes one perspective seem more important than any other. In this, the poem may be said to be related to the proto-cubist and cubist tradition, and to be following the lead of Gertrude Stein in her *Three Lives*. In his essay on Stein, Hubbell glancingly refers to Robert Haas's 1946 interview with her, in which she talks about the importance to her of Cézanne's work:

> Cézanne conceived the idea that in composition one thing was as important as another thing. Each part is as important as the whole, and that impressed me enormously, and it impressed me so much that I began to write *Three Lives* under this influence and this idea of composition. (Transatlantic Interview, 15)

This idea became, I think, equally important to Hubbell. Even though, in the words of Edward F. Fry, 'there always remained in Cézanne's art a strong residue of visual empiricism' (Fry, 14), nevertheless, one brushstroke in Cézanne's work is as important as the next one, both in its relation to other individual brushstrokes, and also – even while it contributes to the coherence of the work as a whole – because it is not subordinated to 'the spatial illusionism of one-point perspective' (Fry, 13), but rather retains its own autonomy as an individual gesture: 'each part is as important as the whole.' This approach to painting contributes, as Fry puts it, to the way that 'objects in paintings of Cézanne assume a … non-perspectival form as a result of multiple perceptions from discrete points of view, accumulated and then expressed in a single composite shape' (Fry, 37). Similarly, each motif in Hubbell's poem – whether dinosaur, delicatessen, or Duchamp's valise – has a value equal to that of all the others both in itself and in its relationship to the formal frame of the whole work; no motifs are pushed into receiving greater or lesser significance by realist devices that aim to create a single position from which the reader views the work. Parataxis is all, and the poem is indeed, to repeat Fry's words, a matter of 'multiple perceptions from discrete points of view, accumulated and then expressed in a single composite shape'.

Hubbell's triptych, being a poem rather than a prose fiction, seems at first to be a very different kind of writing from Stein's *Three Lives* – it has no characters in the way that Stein's short story cycle does, and it is an assemblage of traditional poetic forms rather than a flow of prose marked by syntactic simplicity, circuitous repetition, and incremental variation. Underlying these obvious differences, however, there are some deeper similarities, and it may be that in this poem Hubbell was finally able to deploy what he had learnt from his long-term reading of, and enthusiasm for, Stein's work. It may even be that the basic idea of the triptych was suggested to Hubbell by the three-part structure of Stein's *Three Lives*, just as this work of Stein's had been influenced by Flaubert's *Trois Contes*, which she had been translating at around the time that she started work on her own short story cycle (Haselstein, 388-91).

More important, though, is the parallelism between the three parts that is the key to the structure of both Stein's and Hubbell's works. In Hubbell's case, the parallelism consists of poetic forms deployed in a fixed order while in Stein's case the parallelism that links the three stories is both narrative and thematic. The three lives are parallel in that all three characters live and work in the same town, Bridgeport, and all three of them are working-class women, even if the leading figure in the central story of the triptych, Melanctha, is Black, while the Good Anna and the Gentle Lena, the two framing figures in the shorter first and third stories, are of German immigrant origin. All three stories themselves have a three-part structure, made explicit by the three section headings that appear in the first story: 'Part I', in which the text opens *in medias res*; the biographical 'Part II: The Life of the Good Anna'; and the concluding 'Part III: The Death of the Good Anna'. The second and third stories have the same structure even if they lack the section headings. There are also thematic parallels: for example, all three stories pay close attention to friendships, especially between women, describing a series of relationships which sometimes shade into intimacy and sometimes do not; the three stories also highlight the lack of fulfilment in all three lives. Clearly the reader is meant to notice these parallels: as Richard Heldrich points out, 'even the title itself, *Three Lives*, begs the reader to compare and contrast the variously described lives in this Bridgepoint community'(343), with the result that each new encounter with a theme is partly interpreted through the lens of the reader's understanding of previous encounters with that theme in the same story or in other stories in the cycle. There is thus an underlying coherence in the work as a whole, but one which does not dilute the particularity of any part of it, and in this way the story cycle functions very much like a cubist painting.

This kind of interaction between coherence and particularity could, I think, equally well describe the modus operandi of Hubbell's triptych. As Fry says with reference to the 'repetition of a phrase with progressive variations' which is a key method in such works of Stein as 'Picasso', 'the parallel with analytical cubism is in fact rather striking' (Fry, 56).[4] In the case of Hubbell the 'repetition with progressive variations' is not a patterning of words or phrases but, on a larger scale, of poetic forms, resulting in radical meetings between different forms, varieties of subject matter, and degrees of emotional weight: each of these contributes to the articulation of a different facet of the neighbourhood in question and helps to create in a time-bound medium an equivalent of the spatial practice of the cubist painter. Comparing Gertrude Stein's work with that of Picasso, Hubbell states, 'as the Cubist painter took an object apart and then reassembled the parts according to a completely autonomous sense of design, so she disintegrated her ideational content and reorganized it into a purely formal design' ('Stein: The First Period', 195). In his own triptych the neighbourhoods of Long Island have been taken apart and the resulting multiple viewpoints have been reorganised into the 'purely formal design' of the poem. The result is a poetic equivalent to the 'whole series of overlapping lines, curves, forms' that Hubbell detects in Duchamp's *Nude Descending a Staircase.*

This is not to imply that the formal design is an abstract one. Although in an analytical cubist painting, the focus is, in Fry's words, on 'the formal language used by the artist to create a highly structured aesthetic object,' at the same time 'it would be incorrect to call [such a] painting an abstraction, since it bears a specific relation to external, visual reality' (20). In Hubbell's case, the reality referred to is Brooklyn and Queens and his personal engagement with neighbourhoods in those boroughs, which provides a focus and a referentiality that enhances our sense of the poem's unity. There are sharply observed references to the actual, inhabited world of 1940s Long Island, as in the description of how, among the 'low and even' houses of Glendale, 'the concrete cylinders of the coal company / Like the columns of Karnak stand above the tracks, / Egyptian and important.' Here, twentieth-century industrial reality and ancient Egyptian grandeur achieve simultaneity though the use of simile, but other historic and prehistoric objects and creatures freely appear in the poem *in propria persona*. Thus, dinosaurs, armoured fish, and prehuman hominids can equally be held in the triptych's frame because such creatures did indeed once inhabit Long Island and the waters around it, and were just as actual as any of the life forms that followed them – a point of at least potential relevance and interest to the human creatures descended from them who now, 'more evolved in mind and sense, / inhabit Glendale'.

In addition to this local reference, which helps to root the poem in the specificities of place, another related feature that strengthens the unity of the work is its autobiographical element. Poems of personal experience are interspersed among poems concerning locality, history, or philosophy, a mingling which further helps to ground the poem as a whole in a sense of lived experience: we have the feeling that we are in the presence of an astute, complex, interested, and variously engaged mind interacting with a many-faceted environment. Many of these personal moments are hard-headed and observant of external reality while others are intensely subjective: 'The earth is parched with summer. / I am parched with desire. / Fall, rain.' However, this is not to suggest that the poem is in any way confessional; rather, this presence of an 'I', whether explicitly signalled by the first-person pronoun or merely implied, creates the sense that there is an invisible magnetic or gravitational field holding the universe of the poem together as entity and system. Stenographers, delicatessens, the Canarsie Indians, Mae West, the great institution of the human heart, Vivekananda, the ancient inhabitants of Germany, gold from Wicklow, Brancusi's bird, and 'the loud bullshitting in the pool rooms and the bowling alleys' of Greenpoint, all of which appear in the first panel of *Long Island Triptych*, are certainly various enough – and each as important as any other, as Stein claimed both details and brush strokes should be – but they are held in a multi-faceted unity not only by the overarching poetic form but by the sense that they are all equally facets of the curiosity, knowledge, and perceptions of an inhabitant of the place named in the poem's title.

This anchoring of the poem in the local and the personal means that, despite the elements of both place and person being deliberately dissociated and recombined, they are recognisable in the same way as are some of the subjects of Picasso's portraits from his analytic cubist period. When compared with contemporary photographs, Daniel-Henry Kahnweiler or Wilhelm Uhde are almost uncannily recognisable in Picasso's 1910 portraits of them even while the painting's two-dimensional planes and facets hover on the very edge of abstraction. According to Fry, it is just this tension between the autonomously aesthetic, the 'internally consistent pictorial structure', on the one hand, and the perceived world on the other, that accounts for the 'persisting fascination' of this kind of painting (Fry, 20).

This tension between representation and abstraction resembles that found both in *Long Island Triptych* and in many works by Stein. It seems to me that Hubbell's poem can well be designated a cubist work since it stands as a self-sufficient verbal object with a rigorous architecture that reveals, emphasises, shapes, and reconciles the heterogeneity of image, anecdote, historical account, and all the other dissociated and recombined elements of three Long Island neighbourhoods and of Hubbell's engagement with them. Thus, even though the poem doesn't look or sound like anything that could have been written by Stein, some of its underlying procedures and strategies suggest that Hubbell may indeed be one of her true disciples.

– Paul Rossiter, *Tokyo, March* 2025

NOTES

[1] More details of Hubbell's biography can be found in the introduction to his *Selected Poems*, published simultaneously with this volume.

[2] The Stein-Hubbell correspondence has been preserved in the Beinecke Rare Book and Manuscript Library at Yale. According to Hubbell himself ('Interview', 62), this correspondence began when Hubbell wrote and published an article about her work which somebody showed to Stein, leading her to contact him. He did in fact write an article about her, but it was not published until much later ('The Plain Edition of Gertrude Stein' *Contempo*, Vol. III, No. 12, 25 October 1933); however, the correspondence from 1928 in the Yale archive supports the narrative given here. Hubbell's letter to Jolas: 15 November 1928, YCAL; MSS 76, Box 111 f. 2261; Stein's note to Hubbell: 12 December 1928. YCAL; MSS 77, Box 10 f. 128. Gertrude Stein and Alice B. Toklas Papers, Yale Collection of American Literature. Beinecke Rare Book and Manuscript Library.

[3] See my introduction to Hubbell's *Selected Poems*, where 'Letter to Gertrude Stein' is discussed in more detail, as are 'Angelology' and 'Five Places', two key poems from the first half of *Long Island Triptych and Other Poems* cited later in this afterword.

[4] An example, from 'Picasso' (1912), of Stein's 'repetition of a phrase with progressive variations': 'Some were certainly following and were certain that the one they were then following was one working and was one bringing out of himself then something. Some were certainly following and certain that the one they were then following was one bringing out of himself then something that was coming to be a heavy thing, a solid thing and a complete thing' (*Writings*, 282).

BIBLIOGRAPHY

All quotations from Lindley Williams Hubbell are from: *The Works of Lindley Williams Hubbell*. Ed. Makoto Ozaki. CD-Rom edition. Kyoto: Iris Press, 2005.

OTHER WORKS

Burleigh, David and Hiroaki Sato (eds.). *Autumn Stone in the Woods: A Tribute to Lindley Williams Hubbell.* Middletown Springs, VT: P.S., A Press, 1997.

Danno, Yoko. 'An Interview.' In Burleigh and Sato (eds.), 57-65.

Fry, Edward F. *Cubism*. London: Thames and Hudson, 1966.

Gordon, David M. 'The Structure of Bunting's Sonatas'. In *Basil Bunting: Man and Poet.* Ed. Carroll F. Terrell. Orono: National Poetry Foundation, 1980, 107–124.

Haselstein, Ulla. 'A New Kind of Realism: Flaubert's *Trois Contes* and Stein's *Three Lives.*' *Comparative Literature* Vol. 61, No. 4 (Fall 2009): 388-399.

Heldrich, Philip. 'Connecting Surfaces: Gertrude Stein's *Three Lives*, Cubism, and the Metonymy of the Short Story Cycle.' *Studies in Short Fiction* Vol. 34, No. 4 (1997): 427-39.

Kenner, Hugh. *The Invisible Poet: T. S. Eliot.* New York: McDowell, Obolensky, 1959.

Moody, A. David. '*Four Quartets*: music, word, meaning and value.' In *The Cambridge Companion to T. S. Eliot.* Ed. A. David Moody. Cambridge: Cambridge University Press, 1994. 142-157.

Rexroth, Kenneth. 'The Cubist Poetry of Pierre Reverdy'. In *World Outside the Window: Selected Essays.* Ed. Bradford Morrow. New York: New Directions, 1987. 252-258.

Richie, Donald. 'On First Meeting LWH.' In Burleigh and Sato (eds.), 3-8.

Stein, Gertrude. 'Vacation in Brittany.' *The Little Review* Vol. 8, No. 2 (Spring 1922): 5-6.

Stein, Gertrude. 'A Transatlantic Interview, 1946'. In *A Primer for the Gradual Understanding of Gertrude Stein*. Ed. Robert Bartlett Haas. Los Angeles: Black Sparrow Press, 1971, 15-35.

Stein, Gertrude. *Writings 1903–1932.* Eds. Catherine R. Stimson and Harriet Chessman. New York: Library of America, 1999.

Yamamoto, Shigeki. 'List of Nō Dramas LWH Saw.' In Burleigh and Sato (eds.), 67-72.

www.ingramcontent.com/pod-product-compliance
Lightning Source LLC
LaVergne TN
LVHW091339190726
843491LV00002B/800

* 9 7 8 4 9 0 7 3 5 9 5 1 5 *